CRABS ARE CRUSTACEANS

CRUSTACEANS

For

Dr. Charles Pascoe

who showed me the power

of the creative process

cv

CRABS ARE CRUSTACEANS

By **Cindy Vining**   Illustrated by **Joe York**

omma productions
Austin, Texas

Some of the poems appearing in this volume were inspired
by creative drama experiences at Zachary Scott Theatre
in Austin, Texas.

Individual Acknowledgements:
Zack Anderson, Jessica Miller, Zach Miller

Design by Gabriel Gorman

Library of Congress Catalog Card Number: 97-92282

ISBN 0-9659436-0-7

Omma Productions
P.O. Box 151284
Austin, TX 78715
(512) 312-1560

Printed in the United States of America

CONTENTS

Nickname

Wrinkle faced
Rolly round
Daytime sleepy
Seldom found

Bristle thistle
Puff and spike
Prickle tickle
In the night

Busy dizzy
Circling fast
Oblong creatures
Running past

Burrow furrow
Root and dig
Sniffle snuffle
Little pigs

Mischief?

A

B

C

Delores deliberately doused the dodging duck.

E

F

Georgia gently joggled the giant jellyfish.

H

I

J

Kurt quickly catapulted the crawling critter.

L

M

N

O

P

Q

R

S

Tipper Tucker tickled turtles to turn them.

U

V

W

X

Y

Zach zapped zebras with zipped zippers.

The Dog I Didn't Like

He came each day
And ate the food
I set out for my dog.
My dog stepped back
And let him eat his fill.

He tipped the can
That held my garbage
To see what he could find.
My dog looked on
And let him claim the tasty prize.

He came to lay
Right in the pool
I'd filled up for my dog.
My dog moved over
So they could both enjoy the cool water.

He came one day
With lifted paw
And looked at me for help.
My dog watched me.
I bent down and took out the sharp sticker.

Licking Ice Cream from the Box

Pleasures there are many

In this world of dirt and rocks,

But none is as sweet

As licking ice cream from the box.

Consider

Consider the lowly worm.
It eats the dirt
And expels the dirt
And is none the worse
For having done it.
In fact, it feeds
The very ground
That keeps me alive.

Natural Things

We saw her bring
A piece of string
And add it to the nest.
We all agreed
The thing we see'd,
It was a natural thing.

We watched her sit
And not fidget
For hours upon end.
We all remarked
She liked her part.
It was a natural thing.

We heard the peeps.
We saw the beaks
Open wide for food.
We caught a look,
She didn't cook.
It was a natural thing.

We stepped around
The growing mound
Underneath the nest.
We squealed oooo,
But still we knew,
It was a natural thing.

We saw them grow
And want to go
Away from the nest.
We cheered them on
Though they'd be gone.
It was a natural thing.

Crabs are Crustaceans

Crabs are crustaceans.

It's very plain to see.

Crabs are crustaceans.

They live in the sea.

If I could talk to them,

I'd ask them to swim with me!

But no.

Crabs are crustaceans.

Unlike me.

Cat

Meowing yowling
Catterwallerwowling
Telling me a story
Cat

Purring murring
Kittirillirurring
Saying that he likes me
Cat

Hissing flissing
Felinetailisflicking
Better move away from the
Cat

16

Sometimes

Sometimes the best
Thing to do
Is nothing

When it's
Tongue-hangin' hot

When there's
Nothin' to chase

When the bone
Is under your paw

Sometimes the best
Thing to do
Is nothing

A Short Story

Two good and furry animals
Met in a field one day.
One said to the other,
"I'm hungry, so I'm going to eat you up."

Well, the claws ripped and the fur flew,
And then the next thing you knew,
They stopped.
And one said to the other,
"We're both good and furry animals.
I'm finding something else to eat."

Walk Awhile

I want to walk with you awhile
You look interesting
And I am bored.
So I'll leave my yard
And follow you down the street
Until it feels like I've gone far enough.
Then I'll turn around and go back home.

A Little Something

Leave a little something behind
To show you've passed this way
A note to those who follow
That you had something to say

Some may linger by it
Trying to decode
And some may add to it
Before they move on down the road

The Lion Limerick

There once was a lion I knew
Who lived all of his days at the zoo
When the day to go free
At last came to be
He didn't know what to do

Feelers

Feelers feeling

Things unseen

Vibrate

With delicate accuracy

Detecting

Friends and enemies,

Narrow places,

And the way home.

How Do You Know?

Spider, spider
Weaving your web
Round and round
You spin your thread.
How do you know
Which way to go
When you weave your web?

Wild geese, wild geese
Flying so high
Make a pattern
In the sky.
How do you know
Which way to go
When you fly so high?

Earth worm, earth worm
Under the ground
Making tunnels
All around.
How do you know
Which way to go
When you're under the ground?

Swishers

Two horses

Bothered by flies

Stood side by side

Heads matched to tails

And managed to shoo

The bothersome flies

Away.

Just Another Mule

I may look like
Just another mule
Buckling under the weight
Of someone else's baggage.

But I'm really
A wild stallion
Waiting for a reason
To buck it loose
And gallop into the sunset.

Link

What do you mean
I'm supposed to eat that
And you are supposed to eat me
And the one over there is supposed to eat you?

I'm breaking out of this chain!

Perspective

A wild one said to a tame one,
    "Don't you ever wish to just go
    where you want to go?"

So the tame one said,
    "Don't you ever wish to just be fed
    twice a day every day?"

To which the wild one replied,
    "At least I have the
    opportunity to
    exercise my
    instincts."

And the tame one retorted,
    "At least I don't have to be
    constantly wary."

Then the wild one thought but did not say
    that it would like to know
    a predictable day.

And the tame one thought but did not say
    that it felt at times
    like running away.

The Sentinel

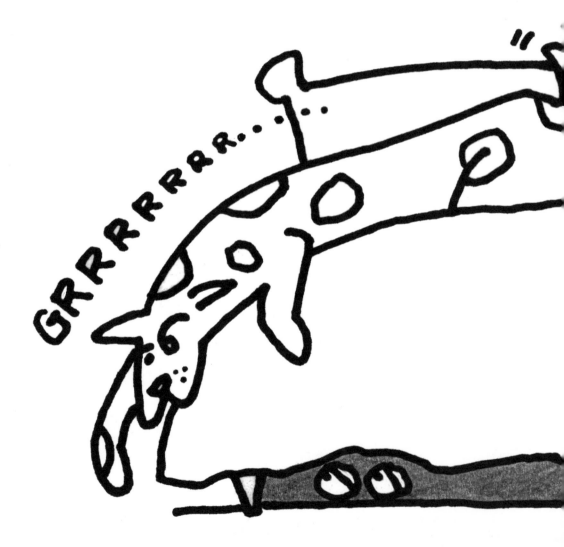

I won't go to bed.
I don't like the dark.
The monsters come out
And the wild howling starts.
Something quite creepy
Crawls from under my bed.
It oozes unspeakable sights
That go into my head.
And there's a creaking from my closet
That causes me alarm.
  I know it's a skeleton ghost
        Intent on my harm.
        Then there's the tapping on my window
        From the long sharp fingernails
    Of that beastly old witch
   With the slime and the scales.
  They all want to eat me,
 I can feel it in my bones!
 I can't go to bed,
I'll be all alone.
  I'll be shredded and torn
    From limb to limb.
      Then they'll all gather around
      To nibble my skin!
        And that's how you'll find me
          When the night finds the day.
          And then won't you be sorry...
          What's that you say?
                Sparky can stay?
                  Thank you.
                    And good night.
                        Come on, Sparky.

40

Master of Disguise

You master of disguise you
Hanging on the wall
Like a miniature exotic mask
When all you are
Is a silly little beetle

Night Whistler

Beautiful in the night
Bird music bright
I thought as I lay myself down

A melodic delight
To say goodnight
I thought as I settled for sleep

Oh it'll be alright
It will take flight
I thought as I tossed and turned

This is starting to bite
I'm ready to fight
I thought as I picked up my shoe

It will squack in fright
When I catch sight
I thought as I charged through the door

Ancient Eyes

Old, old secrets from the sea
Look through your eyes
When you look at me.

Sea to land and land to sea
Have you seen everything
There is to see?

Shied at the Bridge

Down the long and dusty road
Horse and rider sped
Straight and without wavering
They were purpose fed

They'd crossed a burning desert
And miles of razor thorn
Through all kinds of peril
Passed some who'd heaped them scorn

When the sweet smell of water
Wafting gently in the breeze
Caused them to anticipate
Their thirst soon would ease

Then the road went steeply downward
Headlong they ventured still
To the final obstacle
At the bottom of the hill

There was a bridge across
Standing solid in the mist
But a sign along the top read
Cross at Your Own Risk

They stood in heavy silence
Considering the odds
Knowing fully well
Some would name them frauds

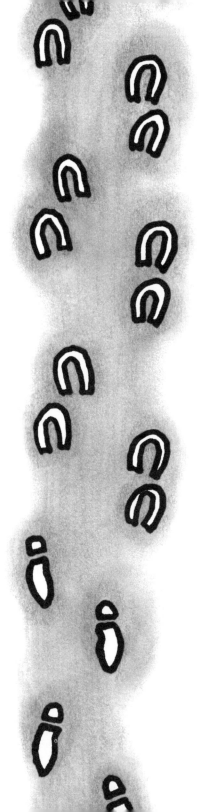

The rider then dismounted
And let go of the reins
One crossed and one did not
And they never met again

Try never to be
The bait.

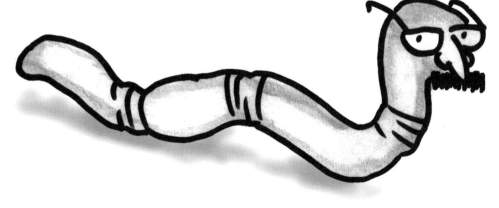